JOURNAL

OUR DAILY BREAD

SOJOURN OF THE SOUL

Discovery House.
from Our Daily Bread Ministries

Discovery House is affiliated with Our Daily Bread Ministries, Grand Rapids, Michigan.

Requests for permission to quote from this book should be directed to: Permissions Department, Discovery House, P.O. Box 3566, Grand Rapids, MI 49501, or contact us by e-mail at permissionsdept@dhp.org.

All Scripture quotations, unless otherwise indicated, are taken from the Holy Bible, New International Version®, NIV®. Copyright © 1973, 1978, 1984, 2011 by Biblica, Inc.™ Used by permission of Zondervan. All rights reserved worldwide. www.zondervan.com. The "NIV" and "New International Version" are trademarks registered in the United States Patent and Trademark Office by Biblica, Inc.™

Cover and interior design by Stan Myers

Photo credits:
  Cover: Terry Bidgood
  Interior:
    ©pidjoe/Gettyimages, Wikimedia Commons
    ©Srdjan Srdjanov/Gettyimages, LiliGraphie, arkbird77/Thinkstock
    ©Cora Niele/Gettyimages, Thinkstock
    ©lysvik photos/Gettyimages, Hemera Technologies/Thinkstock
    ©Terry Bidgood/Our Daily Bread Ministries, Wikimedia Commons
    ©Medioimages/Photodisc, pavila/Thinkstock
    ©Terry Bidgood/Our Daily Bread Ministries, Wikimedia Commons
    ©Terry Bidgood/Our Daily Bread Ministries, pavila/Thinkstock, Wikimedia Commons
    ©John Elk III/Gettyimages, prapann/Thinkstock
    ©SharonKennedy, yangzai/Thinkstock
    ©hanule photography/Gettyimages, BSANI, 100kers/Thinkstock, Wikimedia Commons
    ©Brandon Goldman/Gettyimages, yangzai, koosen/Thinkstock
    ©Terry Bidgood/Our Daily Bread Ministries, Thinkstock

ISBN: 978-1-62707-415-5

Printed in the United States of America
First printing in 2015

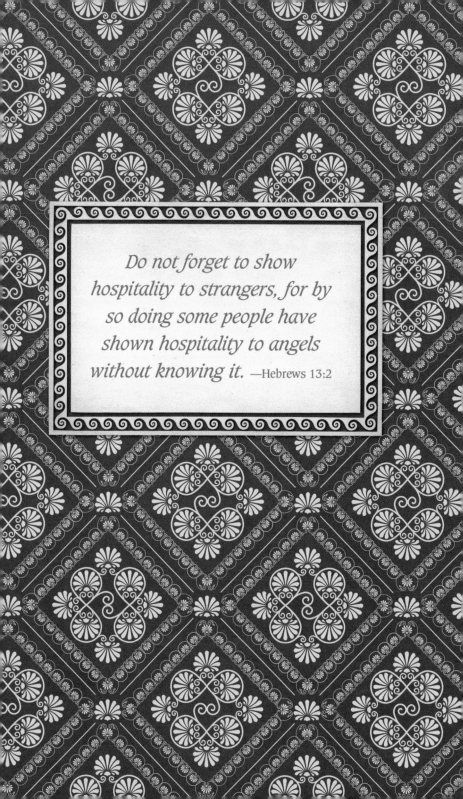

Do not forget to show hospitality to strangers, for by so doing some people have shown hospitality to angels without knowing it. —Hebrews 13:2

*The Mighty One, God, the LORD, speaks and summons
the earth from the rising of the sun to where it sets.*
Psalm 50:1

The heavens declare the glory of God; the skies proclaim the work of his hands.
Psalm 19:1

His name alone is exalted; his splendor is above the earth and the heavens.
Psalm 148:13

All the earth bows down to you; they sing praise to you.
Psalm 66:4

I will walk among you and be your God, and you will be my people.
Leviticus 26:12

In you our ancestors put their trust; they trusted and you delivered them.
Psalm 22:4

From his abundance we have all received one gracious blessing after another.

—John 1:16 (NLT)

This is what the LORD says: "Stand at the crossroads and look; ask for the ancient paths, ask where the good way is, and walk in it, and you will find rest for your souls."
Jeremiah 6:16

*Whether you turn to the right or to the left, your ears will hear a voice
behind you, saying, "This is the way; walk in it."*
Isaiah 30:21

Your word is a lamp for my feet, a light on my path.
Psalm 119:105

The ways of the LORD are right; the righteous walk in them.
Hosea 14:9

The LORD makes firm the steps of the one who delights in him.
Psalm 37:23

When my spirit grows faint within me, it is you who watch over my way.
Psalm 142:3

*They feast on the abundance of your house;
you give them drink from your river of
delights. For with you is the fountain of life;
in your light we see light.*

—Psalm 36:8–9

GUILDFORD
8 30PM
16 AUG
1957
A

GT. BRITAIN

In their hearts humans plan their course, but the LORD establishes their steps.
Proverbs 16:9

The LORD will watch over your coming and going both now and forevermore.
Psalm 121:8

Let us run with perseverance the race marked out for us, fixing our eyes on Jesus, the pioneer and perfecter of faith.
Hebrews 12:1–2

Walk in the way of love, just as Christ loved us and gave himself up for us.
Ephesians 5:2

Wait for the LORD; be strong and take heart and wait for the LORD.
Psalm 27:14

I lift up my eyes to the mountains—where does my help come from? My help comes from the LORD, the Maker of heaven and earth.
Psalm 121:1–2

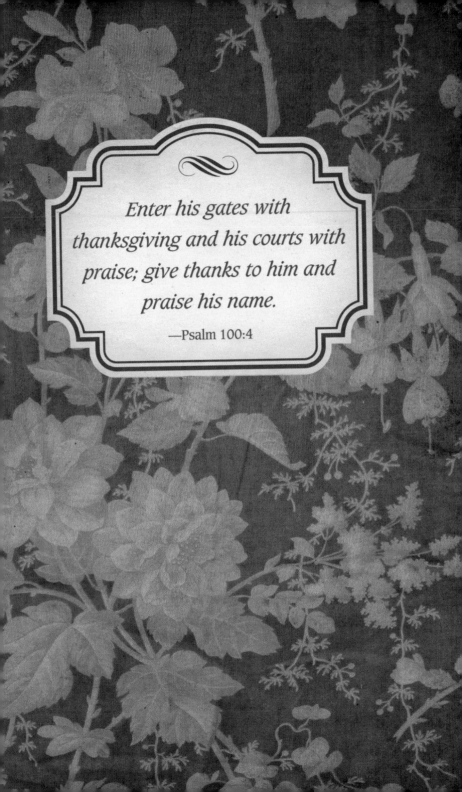

Enter his gates with thanksgiving and his courts with praise; give thanks to him and praise his name.

—Psalm 100:4

Even though I walk through the darkest valley, I will fear no evil, for you are with me.
Psalm 23:4

The LORD watches over all who love him.
Psalm 145:20

Those who hope in the LORD will renew their strength. They will soar on wings like eagles; they will run and not grow weary, they will walk and not be faint.
Isaiah 40:31

The LORD loves righteousness and justice; the earth is full of his unfailing love.
Psalm 33:5

Cast your cares on the LORD and he will sustain you.
Psalm 55:22

Do not worry about tomorrow, for tomorrow will worry about itself.
Matthew 6:34

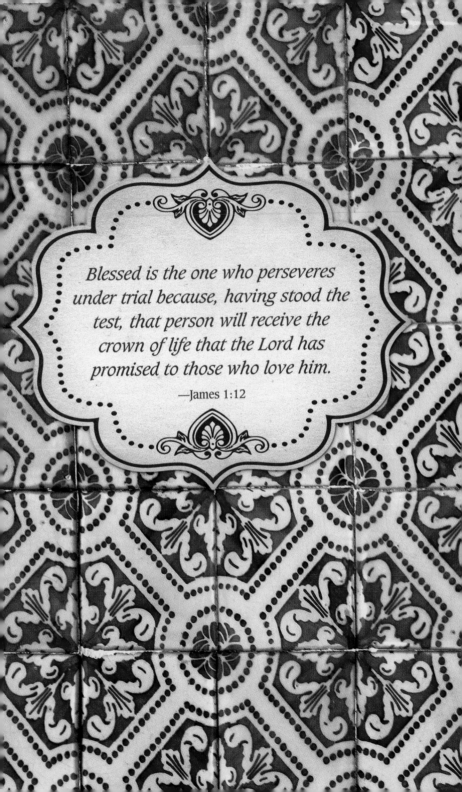

Blessed is the one who perseveres under trial because, having stood the test, that person will receive the crown of life that the Lord has promised to those who love him.

—James 1:12

Come to me, all you who are weary and burdened, and I will give you rest.
Matthew 11:28

I am the way and the truth and the life. No one comes to the Father except through me
John 14:6

As far as the east is from the west, so far has he removed our transgressions from us.
Psalm 103:12

B. & C. D. Ry.
One Day Excursion
BELFAST to HELEN'S BAY
AND RETURN
THIRD CLASS
FOR CONDITIONS SEE BACK

07642

How priceless is your unfailing love, O God! People take refuge in the shadow of your wings. They feast on the abundance of your house; you give them drink from your river of delights. For with you is the fountain of life.
Psalm 36:7–9

I have come that they may have life, and have it to the full.
John 10:10

Love the LORD, all his faithful people! The LORD preserves those who are true to him.
Psalm 31:23

Wait for the LORD; be strong and take heart and wait for the LORD. —Psalm 27:14

CREGNESH
5 PM
12 June
1948
ISLE OF MAN

Come with me by yourselves to a quiet place and get some rest.
Mark 6:31

I rejoiced with those who said to me, "Let us go to the house of the LORD."
Psalm 122:1

He has shown you, O mortal, what is good. And what does the LORD require of you? To act justly and to love mercy and to walk humbly with your God.
Micah 6:8

I heard the voice of the Lord saying, "Whom shall I send? And who will go for us?"
And I said, "Here am I. Send me!"
Isaiah 6:8

Jesus said to his disciples, "Whoever wants to be my disciple must deny themselves and take up their cross and follow me."
Matthew 16:24

The Word became flesh and made his dwelling among us. We have seen his glory, the glory of the one and only Son, who came from the Father, full of grace and truth.
John 1:14

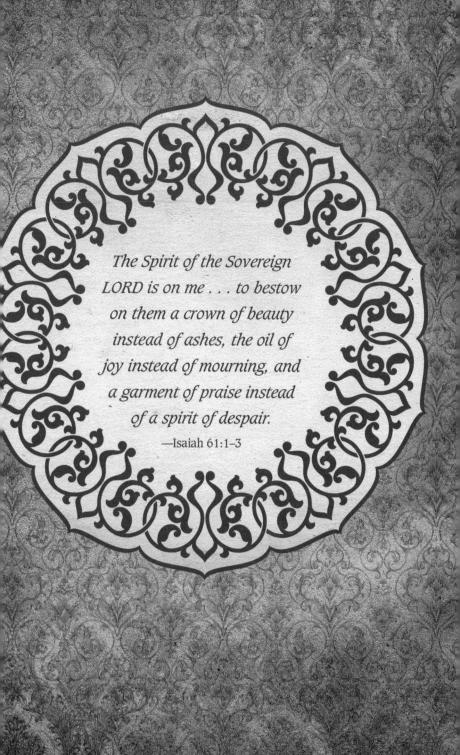

The Spirit of the Sovereign LORD is on me . . . to bestow on them a crown of beauty instead of ashes, the oil of joy instead of mourning, and a garment of praise instead of a spirit of despair.

—Isaiah 61:1–3

Forgetting what is behind and straining toward what is ahead, I press on toward the goal to win the prize for which God has called me heavenward in Christ Jesus.
Philippians 3:13–14

Go and make disciples of all nations, baptizing them in the name of the Father and of the Son and of the Holy Spirit, and teaching them to obey everything I have commanded you. And surely I am with you always, to the very end of the age.
Matthew 28: 19–20

I have fought the good fight, I have finished the race, I have kept the faith.
2 Timothy 4:7

He who was seated on the throne said, "I am making everything new!"
Revelation 21:5

For we live by faith, not by sight.
2 Corinthians 5:7

In all your ways submit to him, and he will make your paths straight.
Proverbs 3:6

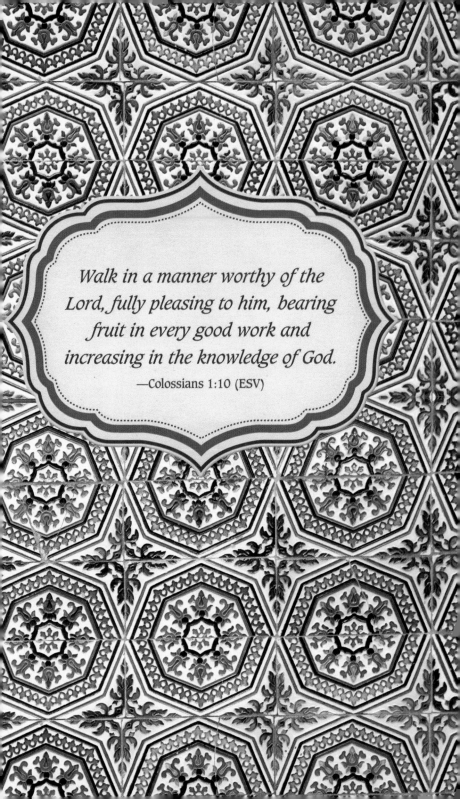

Walk in a manner worthy of the Lord, fully pleasing to him, bearing fruit in every good work and increasing in the knowledge of God.
—Colossians 1:10 (ESV)

Tarjeta Postal

(UNION POSTAL UNIVERSAL)
ESPAÑA

CORREOS
8.4.1932
(AL)
CÓRDOBA

ESPAÑ
3

Ernst Schultze

Kochstr. 44/5 1 Treppe

SW 68

Teach me your way, LORD; lead me in a straight path.
Psalm 27:11

I know what it is to be in need, and I know what it is to have plenty.
I have learned the secret of being content in any and every situation,
whether well fed or hungry, whether living in plenty or in want.
Philippians 4:12

He makes me lie down in green pastures,
he leads me beside quiet waters, he refreshes my soul.
Psalm 23:2–3

We wait in hope for the LORD; he is our help and our shield.
Psalm 33:20

Though I walk in the midst of trouble, you preserve my life.
Psalm 138:7

If I rise on the wings of the dawn, if I settle on the far side of the sea,
even there your hand will guide me, your right hand will hold me fast.
Psalm 139:9–10

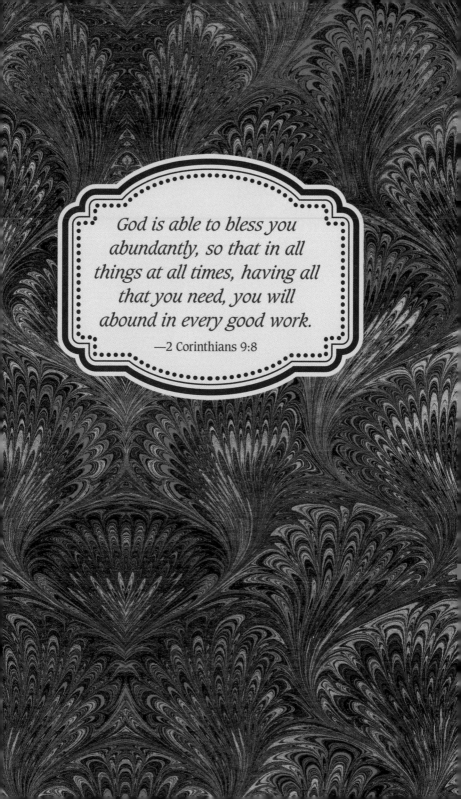

God is able to bless you abundantly, so that in all things at all times, having all that you need, you will abound in every good work.

—2 Corinthians 9:8

Observe the commands of the LORD your God,
walking in obedience to him and revering him.
Deuteronomy 8:6

Since we live by the Spirit, let us keep in step with the Spirit.
Galatians 5:25

Direct my footsteps according to your word; let no sin rule over me.
Psalm 119:133

You have delivered me from death and my feet from stumbling,
that I may walk before God in the light of life.
Psalm 56:13

All the nations may walk in the name of their gods,
but we will walk in the name of the LORD our God for ever and ever.
Micah 4:5

Many peoples will come and say, "Come, let us go up to the mountain of the LORD, to the temple of the God of Jacob. He will teach us his ways, so that we may walk in his paths."
Isaiah 2:3

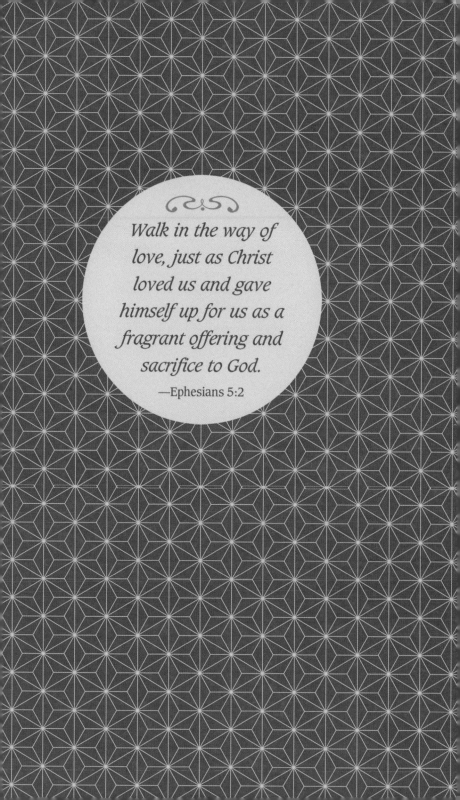

Walk in the way of love, just as Christ loved us and gave himself up for us as a fragrant offering and sacrifice to God.

—Ephesians 5:2

One thing I ask from the LORD, this only do I seek:
that I may dwell in the house of the LORD all the days of my life,
to gaze on the beauty of the LORD and to seek him in his temple.
Psalm 27:4

The city does not need the sun or the moon to shine on it, for the glory of God gives it light, and the Lamb is its lamp. The nations will walk by its light.
Revelation 21:23–24

To this you were called, because Christ suffered for you,
leaving you an example, that you should follow in his steps.
1 Peter 2:21

*Godliness with contentment is great gain. For we brought
nothing into the world, and we can take nothing out of it.*
1 Timothy 6:6–7

*"Do not worry, saying, 'what shall we eat?' or 'What shall we drink?'
or "What shall we wear?' For the pagans run after all these things,
and your heavenly Father knows that you need them. "*
Matthew 6:31–32

"Consider the ravens: They do not sow or reap, they have no storeroom or barn;
yet God feeds them. And how much more valuable you are than birds!"
Luke 12:24

E 2482

OUT	IN
Mon.	Mon.
Tues.	Tues.
Wed.	Wed
Thur.	Thur.
Fri.	Fri.
Sat.	Sa

PREMIER TRAVE
— LTD —

Bell Punch Co., Ltd., Lor

A friend loves at all times,
and a brother is born for
a time of adversity.

—Proverbs 17:17

Do not be anxious about anything, but in every situation, by prayer and petition, with thanksgiving, present your requests to God.
Philippians 4:6

Yes, my soul, find rest in God; my hope comes from him.
Psalm 62:5

In peace I will lie down and sleep, for you alone, LORD, make me dwell in safety.
Psalm 4:8

In six days the LORD made the heavens and the earth, the sea,
and all that is in them, but he rested on the seventh day.
Exodus 20:11

It is good to wait quietly for the salvation of the LORD.
Lamentations 3:26

"Be still, and know that I am God."
Psalm 46:10

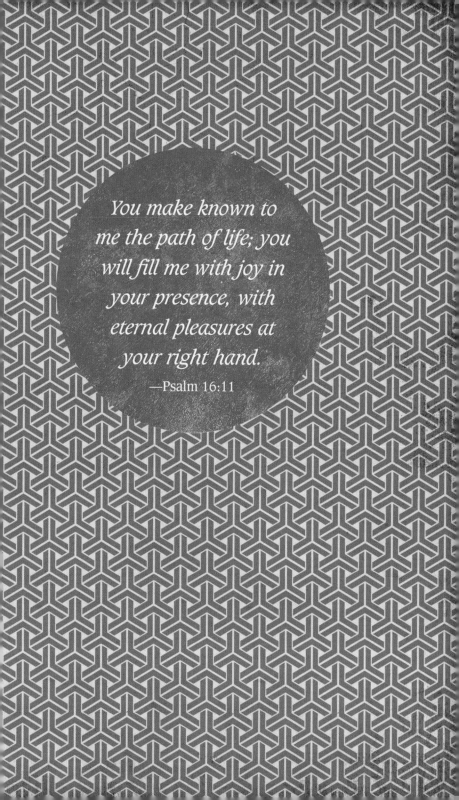

You make known to me the path of life; you will fill me with joy in your presence, with eternal pleasures at your right hand.

—Psalm 16:11

I wait for the LORD, my whole being waits, and in his word I put my hope.
I wait for the LORD more than watchmen wait for the morning.
Psalm 130:5–6

You must return to your God; maintain love and justice, and wait for your God always
Hosea 12:6

Be still before the LORD and wait patiently for him.
Psalm 37:7

Be patient, then, brothers and sisters, until the LORD's coming.
See how the farmer waits for the land to yield its valuable crop,
patiently waiting for the autumn and spring rains.
James 5:7

As for me, I watch in hope for the LORD, I wait for God my Savior.
Micah 7:7

Put your hope in the LORD both now and forevermore.
Psalm 131:3